Love and Memory

by Elizabeth Cogliati

Table of Contents

The Green Hills Far Away

Breath

Out driving with my girl
In the hills east of town
Through the glowing afternoon
The sunlight reflects from storm clouds
Gathering over the mountains
Over the hills invisibly flowing and crumpling
Higher, ever higher. When we are gone past memory,
Mountains will rise here.
Crow lifts off from a fencepost,
Dives into the wheat field, no longer seen.
Sunlight slides into storm,
Our time here is as fleeting as a breath.

Geese

A sudden clatter above – the sound of changing seasons
I rush outside and stare up at the clouds
Circling high above in the misty gray sky,
The geese are gathering on the river.

I rush outside and stare up at the clouds
The geese are calling, gyring to the south
They are gathering over the river.
In the cool air, promising rain, they circle

The geese are calling, gyring to the south
Calling more geese to the circle with every honk,
In the cool air, promising rain, they circle.
The great circle forms a vee, pointing south.

Calling more geese to the circle with every honk,
They are ready – southern grainfields beckon.
The great circle forms a vee, pointing south
Geese sense the earth turning, bringing the cold winter

Circling high above in the misty gray sky
A sudden clatter of honks – the sound of changing seasons
They are ready – southern grainfields beckon
Geese sense the earth turning, bringing the cold winter.

Thieves

Before white men roamed this river valley of hills
Before the wild horses raced across the land
Before wheels cut the grass and plows tore it apart
This land was meant for another people.

In the old land, east of the sea,
Food was scarce and beliefs died for
My kin came here for a new beginning
I cannot go. The old land holds nothing.

The red ones miss me like fish miss water.
How can they be happy when love is gone?
I didn't choose to be born here.
I own this land – I belong now.

Thief, whispers the land. You do not belong to me.
I will not leave my land.

Ohio Lost

Home was the green hills far away
She thought constantly to return
And never thought to stay
Long from the maple and the fern

The brightly shimmering blue day,
The dark, muddy river
Near houses of brown clay
Desert going on forever

Haunted her thoughts by night and day
Longing for home, she dreamed
Cool rivers, falling spray
Hidden deer and huge trees misted

Home was the green hills far away,
She never dreamed she would stay.

The Day

Under the brilliant sky
The land stretches out with no trees by
To support the heavy, blue weight
Tucked into the curve of the hill,
The little cabin sat, still.

She looked out the bare window
Still no neighbors today.
There never would be, here below
This barren hill away
From the mines and churches of town.

What did Jesse want here?
She wondered. It wasn't much of a farm
Or mine. A spasm of fear
Crossed her face and shivered her arms.
How long could she go on?

The door of the cabin slammed open.
A big, red-faced man barged in.
"What, no dinner ready? How can
I work? This is no life for a man!"

She turned away, heavy on her feet
And out, into the heat.

Singing Together

Sunday Singing

Singing together, voices rise in
Community and harmony
Sharing a song, sharing worship
Perfect communion of life, love, and spirit

Community and harmony
Binding together these people in this building
Perfect communion of life, love, and spirit
For these few precious Sunday moments.

Binding together these people in this building
Setting aside all differences
For these few precious Sunday moments
Blending voices in songs of love

Sharing a song, sharing worship
Singing together, voices rise in
Setting aside all differences,
Blending voices in songs of love.

Sing of Living, Sing of Dying

Songs of ancestors echo our lives
Voices of the dead and people mingle
Call and response – hear the answer and ask
Telling the stories of tribal memory
Voices of the dead and people mingle
We are your future being manifest
Telling the stories of tribal memory
Bringing your lives through the coming darkness
Telling the stories of tribal memory
We are now what we will become
Voices of the dead and people mingle
Tell us who went before, for remembrance
We are your future being manifest
Sing us through the ages, taking us home
Bringing our lives through the coming darkness
A sacred responsibility
We are our future, being manifest
Do this in memory of us, the living
Tell us who went before, for remembrance
We are your voices, do not forget us.
Call and response, hear the answer and ask
Sing us through the ages, carrying us home
Songs of the ancestors echo our lives
Do this in memory of us, the dead.

Dreaming with Eyes Wide Open

In the long grass

Dead feather bundle
Dried under the grass, fragile
Sightless eyes and beak

Winter in the Cemetery

The snow falls down, drifting softly over
Grass and headstones, trees and graves, covering
The ache of grief under a cold blanket.
Healing comes slowly to those still living.

Desert Fear

I dreamed a dream, I thought.
Deep in the ravaged desert
Blood stains the soil deep
Child slaves

Deep in the ravaged desert
The cries carry far but no one hears
Child slaves
I forgot as I would a dream but it was real.

The cries carry far but no one hears
Women raped and left to die
I forgot as I would a dream but it was real.
Wide eyes haunt me.

Women raped and left to die
Blood stains the soil deep.
I dreamed a dream, I thought.
Wide eyes haunt me.

Lament

Chorus, chanting
The Dream
(Refrain)
 Lantern flickers
And light falls back
Revealing them
Black as a moon-dark night
        Reaching for him,
            Clawing, grabbing
Light flares up orange,
They shrink away.

Waking
My eyes quick open
Sheets twisted wet
        around – it's the dream – why
                vex me nightly?

Why vex him nightly?
Refrain

Sheets twisted wet
A dream of fear has come
        vex me nightly
Dead! in agony they haunt

Dead! in agony they haunt
Refrain

A dream of fear has come
Torment me who did not save you
Dead! in agony they haunt
I was helpless.

He could not help. He was too late.
Refrain

Torment me who did not save you
from agony I cry for you
I was helpless
sobbing

He loves us always and forever.
Refrain

from agony I cry for you
around it's the dream -- why?
I love you always and forever
eyes wide open.

Refrain (softly)

Leave a Dolly

The ghosts of little girls
Wander the roads at night
Crying for their lost lives
Oh, listen to them cry,
The sobbing, murdered girls.
For the lost girls, leave a
Dolly out some rainy
Evening – a night-crying
Girl will gather it with love.

The Man in White

He was never there until the day you weren't
Lurking in the corners of your mind
Now he won't leave you alone
He won't go away and you find

You cannot forget
He was never there until the day you weren't
Hasn't he done enough?
How can you forget?

Now he won't leave you alone
Just when you think you've forgotten
He springs and the nightmares come flooding back
He was never there until the day you weren't

You never expected this,
Perhaps you were in the wrong place at the wrong time
Now he won't leave you alone

Everywhere you turn, there he is
Even when he's not.
He was never there until the day you weren't
Now he won't leave you alone.

The Way We Are

Fighter Planes

Clipping grass, sun shining
      green sheaves fall
            to black blades
A roar from above
      Black insect rising high
            Another – and another!
The sun shines brightly still
      On my chilled, rising skin
            Another – and another!

How?

I met a man who wasn't there
He shook hands like it was a test
And saluted, looking behind me
Have we a right to condemn?
He shook hands like it was a test,
Told me his sanity was saved.
He saluted, looking behind me,
Speaking of mysterious powders.
Told me his sanity was saved –
Now he is a fisher of men –
Speaking of mysterious powders,
And the ministry that saved his life after war
Now he is a fisher of men.
I listened to him talk
Of the ministry that saved his life after war
How can we ask for a man's life?
I listened to him talk,
Tears pricking my eyes.
How can we ask for a man's life?
Ask for bodies, minds, souls, for our comfort?
Tears pricking my eyes
Have we a right to condemn –
Ask for bodies, minds, souls, for our comfort?
I met a man who wasn't there.

Dear John

Moving on, pause for coffee
Been out of the Navy a long time, moving on
Don't really have a place to be
Moving on, pause for coffee
Seen a lot a long time ago in the Navy
Maybe I saw too much – better gone
Moving on, pause for coffee
Been out of the Navy a long time moving on

The Words

Into the light and out again
Carrying the freight and words
The train cars go a-rumbling on
Freight for the lit houses,
Words for night-time runners
Into the light and out again
Painted with care, or quick
Scrawled in a hurry
The train cars go a-rumbling on.
As long-gone Kilroy was,
So these graffiti kids are now.
Into the light and out again
Artists of spray, masters of risk,
Daring the yard boss's anger
The train cars go a-rumbling on
Words disappearing in the night
Revolution alongside order
Into the light and out again
The train cars go a-rumbling on.

Interstate

Diamonds on the road
Flow down the asphalt
Trading partners,
Dancing down the distances
Flow down the asphalt
Passing time with competition
Dancing down the distances
Finessing the interstices
Passing time with competition
Merging boundaries
Finessing the interstices
Creating beautiful patterns.
Merging boundaries
Trading partners
Creating beautiful patterns,
Diamonds on the road.

We Need Gas

We need gas, the tattered sign said
He (holding the sign) had a Mohawk
She was plump and not all that old
He (the other one) was shaggy
They had a dog, a mutt of some kind

The car mightn't get very far
(Even on a full tank of gas)

I wanted to help them
(But I was too afraid)
And so I left them there, alone.

Northgate Mile (The Way We Were)

Coming up the hill in the dusky light
The car headlights catch the shadowed
Old buildings, light up the neon with faded
Memories of color and the windows
Fill with light and flick'ring shadows.

In the flick of light and shadow play
Come the remembered days of glory.

Cars with fins of strong and painted steel
Hold girls and boys neatly dressed who
Hurry through the early evening –
Dinner, a movie at the drive-in.

Gone now, remembered only
In the light of a passing car,
Flick'ring over the old neon.

Come Dance With Me

Dancing in the Woods

Come dance with me
She sees no one, the woods are quiet
A sibilance on the wind
Turning round and round
Searching for the sound
Come dance with me
Come be my queen,
Come away with me.

A sibilance on the wind
She holds out her hands,
Turning slowly in the rising wind
Come dance with me

Still she sees no one
A pressure on her hands
A sibilance on the wind
Whirling faster and faster
She rises into the air and disappears
Come dance with me
A sibilance on the wind.

Dialogue

Do you know who I am?
I am looking for you
Or can you see only a part of me
I confess I cannot see beyond your beauty
Look past the smile
Perhaps I could see you
See me for who I am
If I could see me.

Can you only see a part of me,
I confess I cannot see beyond your beauty
The part you want to see?
*Self-examination is not my fort*e´
See me for who I am
If I could see me
Passionate and loving
The world would be my oyster

The part you want to see
*Self-examination is not my fort*e´
Does not define me
Why ask me questions I cannot answer
Passionate and loving
The world would be my oyster
I am more than you ever expected
If I knew what to say

Do not define me

Why ask me questions I cannot answer
Look past the smile
Perhaps I could see you
I am more than you ever expected
If I knew what to say
Do you know who I am?
I am looking for you.

Falling

Let me tell you a story: what I learned of love

First
He said he was falling so —
Falling into needful lust
He lost all his kindness,
Taking her in shame and power.

Second
He said he was falling so —
Falling into love
It wasn't fair nor right,
Not when he couldn't promise Forever.

Now
I have learned the important thing:
Not the falling
Who catches you when you fall
Forever comes when you catch your love
Your love catches you, turn and turn about.

In the Moment

Within the moment truth
Arises unspeaking and silent
Opens the door to vision
Darkness hangs suspended
Arises unspeaking and silent
Moves shimmering into the world
Darkness hangs suspended
Awaiting the moment
Moves shimmering into the world
Glances become words
Awaiting the moment
The words are yet untrue
Glances become words
Open the door to vision
The words are yet untrue
Within the moment – truth.

The Lost Letter

Written and sent, but lost
Changed the course of his life
An avowal of his love, star-crossed
For the unfaithful one.

Changed the course of his life
Vowing faithfulness forever
For the unfaithful one
He dreamed of his letter every night

Vowing faithfulness forever
Obsessing in his monk's cell of stamps misplaced
He dreamed of his letter every night
Unfaithful in spirit to his vows

Obsessing in his monk's cell of stamps misplaced
An avowal of his love, star-crossed
Unfaithful in spirit to his vows
Written and sent, but lost.

The End

Softly Now

In the quiet room
She sits, hands folded
The mantel clock ticks
The morning passes
She sits, hands folded,
Waiting. She has no worries.
The morning passes.
The sun moves across the floor.
Waiting, she has no worries.
It will be time soon.
The sun moves across the floor.
She closes her eyes.
It will be time soon
The mantel clock ticks
She closes her eyes
In the quiet room.

www.ingramcontent.com/pod-product-compliance
Lightning Source LLC
Chambersburg PA
CBHW030314030426
42337CB00012B/703